VOICES FROM THE SISTERHOOD:
SPIRITUAL REFLECTIONS, VOLUME 1

WORDS OF INSPIRATION AND ENCOURAGEMENT

The Sisterhood
Brooklyn Community Church

D. PULANE LUCAS AND L. PRISCILLA HALL

Photography by Lorraine Gamble-Lofton

Archway Publishing books may be ordered through booksellers or by contacting:

Archway Publishing
1663 Liberty Drive
Bloomington, IN 47403
www.archwaypublishing.com
1-(888)-242-5904

ISBN: 978-1-4808-1364-9 (sc)
ISBN: 978-1-4808-1365-6 (e)

Printed in the United States of America.

Archway Publishing rev. date: 3/4/2015

The purpose of this book is to give voice to African-American Christian women who have shared their thoughts through words and images to encourage all women to speak confidently about the goodness of God.

All photos featured in this book were taken by Brooklyn Community Church Photographer Lorraine Gamble-Lofton at the 2014 Macy's Flower Show in New York City.

Writers:
Tania Ambroise • Leonna Brabham • Antonia H. Daniels • Tahesha Davis • Lorraine Gamble-Lofton • L. Priscilla Hall • Marilyn A. Hunte • Kareema Johnson • Jessica Leach • D. Pulane Lucas • Fred Lucas • Charlene Phillips • Veronica L. Price • Martha Ramsay • E. Frances Reid • Hattie Smith-Harris • Pamela Stanley • Lois Staton-Godwin • Bernadine Thomas-Williams • Vonceil Turner • Angelique Wharton • Belinda Williams • Carolyn R. Williams

Editors: D. Pulane Lucas and L. Priscilla Hall

CONTENTS

VOICES FROM THE SISTERHOOD:
SPIRITUAL REFLECTIONS, VOLUME 1

My prayer is not for them alone. I pray also for those who will believe in me through their message, that all of them may be one, Father, just as you are in me and I am in you.

~John 17:20-21 (NIV)

Embrace Sisterhood
Behold the Glory of the Lord!

Brooklyn Community Church
Rev. Dr. Fred Lucas, Founder and Senior Pastor
Rev. Maurice Douglas, Pastor for Outreach Ministries
Rev. Pamela Stanley, Pastor for Church Administration

THE SISTERHOOD VISION AND MISSION STATEMENTS
(THE WOMEN'S MINISTRY OF BROOKLYN COMMUNITY CHURCH)

". . . that they all may be one. . ."

~John 17:21 (NKJV)

Vision Statement

The Sisterhood is comprised of all women of the Brooklyn Community Church. The organization is coordinated by women and exists to serve women by meeting a myriad of needs, including spiritual, emotional, social, and educational. The Sisterhood aims to achieve 100% active engagement of the women of BCC.

Mission Statement

The mission of The Sisterhood is to bring women closer to Christ through worship, study, service, fellowship and evangelism, while serving God individually and collectively. It is our responsibility to nurture and uplift one another, build trusting relationships, and equip and encourage all women to grow in Christ through expressions of kindness, love, and friendship.

A Word from the Pastor

"But Jesus said, 'No, go home to your family, and tell them everything the Lord has done for you and how merciful he has been'."
~Mark 5:19 (NLT)

On behalf of the leadership and membership of Brooklyn Community Church, I would like to express our gratitude to The Sisterhood for the conception and production of this amazing compilation, *Voices From The Sisterhood: Spiritual Reflections, Vol. 1.* Congratulations for setting a high standard in moving us beyond our treasured "oral tradition" to commit our remembrances and revelations to paper to be shared with the present and unborn generations. I hope that this is just the beginning of the BCC literary tradition.

This publication is a bold and timely collection of the product of the life experiences, sorrows and joys, trials and triumphs, crucifixions and resurrections, perspiration and inspiration of African-American women who are not ashamed to share with us the reality of the "goodness of the Lord in the land of the living." Each in her own unique voice has reminded us that life is not without its struggles, but that ultimate victory belongs to those who faint not.

This labor of love flows out of the initial phase of the launching of our Sisterhood or women's ministry. The effort is a reflection of unity, sharing, and caring of our dynamic and creative sisters who have begun to mobilize their collective forces for a revolution of love in our church, homes and community. These wonderful women hail from all walks of life and diverse backgrounds, yet are united through the bonds of color, culture, and spiritual consciousness.

A special word of gratitude is due to the co-editors, First Lady D. Pulane Lucas and Deacon L. Priscilla Hall. Dr. Lucas, Judge Hall and all contributors have spent innumerable hours toiling at this "peek" into the inner sanctum of their personal relationship with God. As I read, I truly felt privileged and honored.

On behalf of our male elders and young warriors, please let me express a special word of pride for the witness, enduring testimonies, faith and faithfulness of the women of our church. For many years to come, you have truly inspired and encouraged us all.

Your Brother in Christ,

Rev. Dr. Fred Lucas
Founder and Senior Pastor, Brooklyn Community Church

INTRODUCTION

This compilation of spiritual reflections, poems, and other works was collected to capture the excitement, wisdom and spiritual depth of a group of women who joined together to launch the Women's Ministry of Brooklyn Community Church, later named The Sisterhood. Each week we gathered by conference call to coordinate our special days and events—a luncheon, Women's Day Service, a bus trip to shop and see a play, a baked goods auction, Mother's Day Service, and more. Our meetings commenced with one of our sisters reading a scripture, offering reflections on the scripture, and praying. This book offers a glimpse at what we experienced and shares some of the fruits of our labor.

The writers in this volume represent the diverse body of African-American women—some church founders, others new members. Our ages ranged from early 20s to mid-80s. Our reflections are personal and inspirational. For some of us, the contributions represent our first published work. Others are established scholars, educators, and professionals. Together, we work, love, support and honor one another. Together, we are The Sisterhood. Our goal was to create a compilation of spiritual and inspirational reflections rooted in the Black Church worship and fellowship experience, derived from the broad perspective of African-American women. The words in this book reflect our joys, struggles, challenges and thoughts. We are beautiful black women of various hues, shapes, and features. We are spiritually, socially, economically, politically, and intimately woven together by bonds of love, friendship, and respect.

We give thanks to God for our pastor, Rev. Dr. Fred Lucas, and for his vision and leadership. A heartfelt thank you goes to each sister who contributed to the formation of this volume. We sincerely appreciate the time, talent and support of everyone who helped to make our book, *Voices From The Sisterhood*: *Spiritual Reflections, Vol. 1*, a reality.

We give God honor and praise for all that we are and shall be. We are so grateful for His love and ask that He continue to inspire us, encourage us, protect us and bless us as we strive to do His will.

Forever grateful,

D. Pulane Lucas
President, The Sisterhood

L. Priscilla Hall
Vice President, The Sisterhood

WOMEN CALLED TO SPIRITUAL WARFARE

Veronica L. Price

Ephesians 6:12-13

Focal verse: *"Therefore, take up the whole armor of God, that you may be able to withstand in the evil day, and having done all, to stand."*

~Ephesians 6:13 (NKJV)

My reflection turns to the Book of Judges (Chapters 4 and 5) where we read about Deborah, who was the first and only woman judge and leader of the Israelite army. She was known as the "Mother of Israel" because of her leadership in the battle against Canaanite oppression. Sisera was the military commander of the Canaanite army. He was powerful and feared. He led a strong, efficient and well equipped army. However, God had called Deborah to take on and defeat Sisera. Without hesitation, she answered the call, and God allowed her to overcome this powerful opponent. Deborah led her people to an unbelievable victory. This was clearly attributed to her unwavering obedience, faith and trust in God.

Today our enemies are spiritual forces of darkness and principalities. Just as God equipped Deborah with the necessary weapons and armor needed to overcome her physical foe, He has provided us with the necessities to overcome our spiritual enemies. It is important for us to be like Deborah. We must be obedient and have unwavering steadfast faith and trust in God.

As servants of God, we are encouraged to step into the roles for which He has called us. We must use the gifts and talents that he has given to us. We must strengthen our faith in God, and trust in Him to deliver us from our foes, as we serve and lead His people. We must be ready to answer His call on our lives.

Prayer: Father God, we come before you ready to battle in the world. Guide us. We pray that we will be obedient to Your call. In Jesus' name we pray. Amen.

SISTER TO A SISTER
Leonna Brabham

Mercy, mercy, mercy
Judge not thy sisters on the sins they have committed
Instead, praise thy sisters on the deeds they have given
Let the fruits of her hands work as she rises to the gates
Love her for she will love you even more
Strengthen her, as wisdom comes, see the goodness a women has to offer
For she needs you as well as you will need her
God made Man, and then came woman—together they tie the knot
Let us not forget a women's worth, a strong creator proving birth
Juggling many things as she works around the earth
Sister to another sister, I am not here to put you down
Look around, we're gathered together in the name of one God
One Psalm, one sound, one voice
We sing as a choir in harmony, we worship simultaneously in unity, we dance as a group
We are not here to critique you; we are our sisters' keepers!
Proverbs 31:10 asks: "Who can find a virtuous woman? For her price is far above rubies"
Recognize her duties are not as easy as they may seem
Her love is genuine—many call extreme
We've made mistakes and we're sorry for that too, but do not let that haunt us forever
I am my sister's keeper
We shall always be together!

WAIT ON THE LORD

*"In the morning, O Lord, you hear my voice; in the morning I lay
my requests before you and wait in expectation."*

~Psalm 5:3 (NIV)

APPRECIATE LIFE!
Hattie Smith-Harris

Psalm 90:1-15

Focal verse: *"Oh, satisfy us early with Your mercy, That we may rejoice and be glad all our days!"*

~Psalm 90:14 (NKJV)

The meaning of Psalm 90 came to me during my uncle's passing. Verse 10 stood out to me: "For [life] is soon cut off, and we fly away." The Bible says that we can live 70 or 80 years, but this verse helped me understand that we too are here for just a little while.

When I was young, I learned about the Bible and tried to abide by His word. Yet, there are still things that I have to do to get my life in order. When my mother was living and residing in a nursing home, she asked me: "Did I raise you right?" Although I had issues with my mom growing up, I responded, "yes". When we reflect on our lives, it is important that we have lived right. Sometimes I feel sad because I made mistakes in life, and I realize that there is so much that I need to get right. I need to treat people right—the way that I want people to treat me. I am trying to walk right and talk right and live right now. I tell my daughters and family members that I love them. I gain wisdom from the scriptures. When I finish reading His word, I am thankful that God has kept His hand on me.

As I deal with cancer, God knows that I want to live a long life. As I reflect, I ask myself: Are you handling your journey the way God wants you to? How strong is your faith? Can you trust Him? The experience of living with cancer has made me appreciate life. It is time for me to be an example and encourage others to be able to deal with life's challenges. This is particularly important to teach my children and family members. I know in my heart that whatever God has meant for me will happen. I trust and believe in God with all my heart.

Prayer: Dear God, thank you for our loved ones who have helped us to be strong and our ancestors who are with us. Thank you for Brooklyn Community Church. It is one of the best things in my life. Thank you for the ability to appreciate life. Amen.

SISTER LOVE
Vonceil Turner

Hebrews 13:1-3
Focal verse: *"Keep on loving each other as . . . sisters."*
~Hebrews 13:1 (NIV)

One spring morning as I was walking down a Brooklyn street on my way to our Church offices, I noticed a painting in a store window. On the painting was a prayer titled, *Time Well Spent*, by an anonymous author. The words of the prayer caught my attention because they seem to express what our Sisterhood is about. The prayer read:

"Our prayer is that women everywhere will learn to live as sisters, to respect each other's differences, to heal each other's wounds, to promote each other's progress, and benefit from each other's knowledge."

~Author Unknown

Prayer: Dear Heavenly Father, bless our Sisterhood. Allow us to be what you would have us to be. Let our love for You and others be evident to all. In Jesus' name we pray. Amen.

FEAR NOT

"So we say with confidence, The Lord is my helper; I will not be afraid."
~Hebrews 13:6 (NIV)

WOMEN WORKING OUT OUR SALVATION
Martha Ramsay

Philippians 2:12-13

Focal Verse: *"…work out your own salvation with fear and trembling…"*
~Philippians 2:12 (NKJV)

As women, what does it mean to "work out your salvation"? Many people mistakenly think Paul was telling us to work *for* our salvation. But the apostle was saying something completely different. Your salvation experience isn't the end of your spiritual journey. It is the catalyst that turns on your "operation mode".

Having trusted Jesus as Savior, we can begin living out what He has given us, which is His abundant life. If you have given your heart to Him, the Holy Spirit now indwells you; and He is with you forever. God's Spirit is working in and through you, empowering you to live out your salvation. The degree to which you yield to Him impacts the work He will accomplish through you and the changes He will effect in your life. Let's say you start reading the Bible and learning about the Lord. As your faith and relationship with God develop, you will begin to notice Him moving in your life. When you share your faith and your blessings with others, you will realize that He is working through even more avenues. Keep following Him and the seeds He has planted within you will flourish (Isaiah 55:10-11). So when the Scripture speaks about working out our salvation, it means we are to reverently live out what we have already been given through Christ and allow Christ's life in us to come fully to fruition. Our salvation should be a reflection of Jesus everywhere we go. As we work out our salvation among friends and family and even with strangers, God's Spirit will energize us to make a difference in the lives of others—that is, we are to be salt of the earth and light of the world (Matthew 5:13-16).

Prayer: Christ our Savior, we place You at the very center of our lives. We are thankful for every day that God gives us breath. Through you, we are transformed. Thank you for salvation. Amen.

GIVE MERCY

Antonia H. Daniels

Mercy, mercy, mercy
We scream, Lawd have mercy
We pray to the Lord to have mercy
We say Lawd have mercy on her soul
But is it just talk
Is it just something we just say because we're used to saying it
Do we show mercy to our sisters
Do we reach out to help her when she screams, "Lord have mercy!"
The Lord grants us mercy and shows us mercy
So we can give mercy to others
So instead of asking for mercy
Why don't we reach out and give mercy
Give mercy to that sister who you talked and laughed about behind her back...
And smiled in her face
Give mercy to the sister who can't figure out how to take care of her kids
Give mercy to the sister who's lost and doesn't know where to go
Give mercy to the seasoned sister who just needs a little attention because there is no one else
Give mercy just like God has given His mercy to you

GOD IS MY DRIVER

Jessica Leach

Proverbs 3:5-9

Focal verse: *"In all ways acknowledge Him, And He shall direct thy paths."*

~Proverbs 3:6 (NKJV)

I find it interesting that we are told not to question God, but we are raised to ask questions. We learn and develop by asking questions. Yet, the answers to our questions can leave us feeling insecure when we trust in ourselves and others. Answers can make us feel like failures. Answers can make us think we are alone. But we do not question the air we breathe. We trust that we will breathe another breath.

Being put in difficult situations will cause us to ask: Why God? We must put our trust in God. Nothing that happens to us is by chance. Everything that happens to us is preparation for what He is bringing us to. We have to trust The Lord and not depend on our own knowledge. We must acknowledge God's ways even when we can't see the light. With God we have nothing to fear. Understand He is listening even when He does not say *yes*, *no*, or *ok*. Step out on faith. Trust yourself enough to trust God with ease. God sees all, but we are blessed to see a piece. His right to direct

our lives is way above our right to understand. Patience comes with trusting His word. He does not answer when the clock strikes the closest hour because He does not work on hours, seconds or minutes...but on belief, faith, love and understanding!

Prayer: Dear Lord, help us put our trust in You. Help us lean on Your understanding. God, be our driver. Keep our car safe on the road of our life's journey.

I Love the Lord
Angelique Wharton

Deuteronomy 6:5
Focal Verse: *"And thou shalt love the LORD thy God with all thine heart, and all thy soul, and all thy might."*

~Deuteronomy 6:5 (KJV)

When I started doing research for my Bible scripture, I was unsure about which scripture to select. There were so many that I liked, and they were all so powerful and meaningful. I spoke to my dad about my situation, and he suggested that I think about Deuteronomy 6:5, where it reads: "Love the Lord thy God with all of your heart. . . ." I was like, okay; I like this one.

But then I started to really think about what my dad had said to me. You see, my dad knows me. He knows my life, my struggles and my triumphs. He knows and loves me. Thinking about my father's love for me made me think about my love for my son and daughters. And I asked myself: Do you love the Lord as much as you love them? Well, the answer is YES! Can I love myself and my children more than I love the Lord? The truth is I can't. I love the Lord with a passion. If I didn't, I wouldn't have my children. I wouldn't have a family, and I wouldn't have a life—at least not a fulfilling one. The Lord is my strength and my salvation. I turn to Him in good times and the bad times. Yes, I love the Lord with all my heart, soul and might. And I will continue to do so here and ever after.

Prayer: Heavenly Father, thank you for first loving us and showing us how to love. By Your example, we learn to love others. Our love for You helps us serve You and enjoy the benefits of knowing a good God. Amen.

LOVE
Bernadine Thomas-Williams

1 Corinthians 12:31 and 13:1-3
Focal verse: *"If I speak in the tongues of men or of angels, but do not have love, I am only a resounding gong or a clanging cymbal."*
~1 Corinthians 13:1 (NIV)

The author of this letter was Paul who was becoming aware of the struggles of the Christians in Corinth. Paul aims to show the Corinthians how useless the spiritual gifts are without love. Although there is a diversity of spiritual gifts, love is the most important spiritual gift. It does not matter who you are, your degrees, position or status, love is the gift that is accessible to all. Love is the power activator of all spiritual gifts. Without love, actions and attitudes have no validity.

Remember, God commands us to love. If He commands us to love, then it is in our power to love. God is love. Look to the cross (Golgotha/Calvary) which is all about love.

Prayer: Dear Heavenly Father, teach us humility and love that looks beyond the faults of others and sees their needs. Help us walk in the spirit to grow to love others. Amen.

No More Tears/Be Encouraged

Tahesha Davis

Revelation 21:1-5

Focal verse: *"And God shall wipe away all tears from their eyes and there shall be no more death, neither sorrow, nor crying, neither shall there be any more pain; for the former things are passed away."*

~Revelation 21:4 (KJV)

On July 24, 2012, my husband's birthday, I suffered a miscarriage - one that could have taken me out of this world. The mental, emotional, and physical pain that I endured was almost unbearable. I felt at that point that there was no God. I asked myself: How can God allow me to go through such pain?

There were days when I could not even look at a baby without crying. But in the midst of all of my pain and suffering there was a peace that came over me—the calming spirit of Almighty God. I felt as though God was taking His fingers and wiping away my tears. A still small voice said unto me: "I am here for you, no more tears". God encouraged me and told me to be still and know that He is God. I asked God, Why can't I have children? His reply was: "Not now; it's not the time". As women, we suffer heartaches, miscarriages, and pain, but understand that whatever you are going through you are not alone. God is with you. I am a witness that God will wipe away every tear that you cry and take away every pain that you feel. Be encouraged and know that you can call on God any time—day or night—His line is never busy.

Prayer: Thank you, Father, for all you have done and will do. Wipe away every tear, take away every pain, touch every heart. I ask these things in Jesus' name.

WITH GOD, I AM STRONG

"Do not grieve, for the joy of the Lord is your strength."

~Nehemiah 8:10 (NIV)

GOD IS AMAZING

Kareema Johnson

I thought I couldn't make it through some days, but that never stopped me from giving God praise. Through my darkest hours when I felt overwhelmed, He sent His angels of mercy to comfort and calm me. My God never fails.

When I thought I had no more to give, I was reminded that God gave His son so that I could live. When I was angry and wanted to hold a grudge; I quickly forgave, thinking where would I be without God's love.

Praise will forever be on my tongue. My God is amazing—creator of the moon and sun, heaven, earth, mountains and sea. He's here to protect, direct and guide me. Forgiver of all my sins. I love Him because He first loved me.

He is mighty. King of Kings. Alpha and Omega. Creator of All Things.

Hallelujah is the highest praise! I could never run out of reasons to praise His name.

LA-LA MEANS GOD LOVES YOU

Marilyn A. Hunte

Mark 5:38-42

Focal verse: *"Then He took the child by the hand, and said to her,*
"Talitha cumi," which is translated, 'Little girl, I say to you, arise'."
~Mark 5:41 (NKJV)

Talitha cumi. Even before I knew the translation, I was impressed by the musicality of that phrase. The words sounded melodious and sweet to my ear. Talitha cumi: Aramaic words from the dialect spoken by Jesus. Different versions of the Bible render various translations for 'Talitha cumi.' Little girl, little maid, damsel, get up, wake up, arise. Interested in digging deeper, I looked up 'Talitha cumi' in Hastings' Dictionary of the New Testament. The meaning given there was: "Lambkin, arise." Lambkin. That's not a word I hear every day. Lambkin is a compound word, composed of two words: "lamb" and "kin." Kin means family. The way I see it, here's Jesus, the Lamb of God, referring to us – you and me, as His kin. We are Jesus' family! Hallelujah!

Jesus resurrected Jairus' daughter. This precious little lamb was dead, but with compassion, our miracle-working God brought her back to life. My sisters, have you ever felt dead? Mortally wounded by physical, emotional, financial or spiritual illness? Jesus says to you: "Lambkin arise." You who believe Jesus is the Resurrection and the Life, though you were dead, yet shall you live.

Back in the day, there was a hit R&B song: "La-La Means, I Love You" made popular by the Delfonics. But now I'm hooked on these divine phonics – a spiritual remix: "La-La Means, God loves you." L for Lambkin, A for Arise. L-A spells La. La-La means God loves you.

May the Lord God follow, lead and surround your soul with His love and comfort. Lambkin arise! La-La means God loves you!

Prayer: Eternally Compassionate God, we rejoice that You love us, Abba, Father. Remind us that we are Your lambkins, and we shall overcome death through You, Jesus. Amen!

A Celebration of Sisterhood
Lorraine Gamble-Lofton

Litany

Leader: Precious Lord, today, we lift our celebration of sisterhood to You

People: Today, we celebrate sisterhood.

Leader: Father, give us courage to love and believe in ourselves, faith to trust in Your Love for us and the humility to accept Your will.

People: Please teach us to love, respect and believe in others as we do ourselves.

Leader: Dear God, unite us through worship, study, service, fellowship and evangelism.

People: Thank you Lord for the unifying blessing of sisterhood, "that all may be one".

Leader: Holy Spirit, help us to become more compassionate so that we are better equipped to hear and respond to the needs of others.

People: Lord, empower our Sisterhood to serve You by serving the needs of others.

ALL: Lord, let our love for each other be sacrificial, honest, warm and real. May there be strength in our unity, so that all may be ONE!

REST IN HIM

"Cast all your anxiety on him because he cares for you."
~1 Peter 5:7 (NRSV)

GIRL POWER
Charlene Phillips

Galatians 5:22-23

Focal verse: *"But the Holy Spirit produces this kind of fruit in our lives: love, joy, peace, patience, kindness, goodness, faithfulness, gentleness, and self-control."*

~Galatians 5:22-23 (NLT)

A popular nursery rhyme states: "Sugar and spice and everything nice, That's what girls are made of". We have all heard these words. As children it was always encouraging. There was a smile and a feeling of sweetness. Then we grow up. The very nature of a sisterhood, our Sisterhood, God's sisterhood has a grown up version that is biblically based and irrefutable. So if you find yourself low and depleted, just remember this recipe:

*We give **love** fearlessly*
*We have the **joy** of Jesus to sustain us*
*We present a countenance of **peace** through good and bad times*
*We exhibit **patience** to enable forward mobility*
*We learn **kindness** at the knees of our elders*
*We thrive on **goodness** to help others and ourselves*
*We bask in the glow of **faithfulness** for guidance*
*We add a sprinkle of **gentleness** to soothe aches*
*And we exercise **self-control** to tie it all together*

This is our grown-up version of the sugar and spice nursery rhyme—a Holy Spirit produced fruit, an exceptional gift from God.

As we continue to produce this fruit, we are more than conquerors. As it is written in Psalm 139:14, ". . . for I am fearfully and wonderfully made. . . ."

Let us embrace and share our GIRL POWER!

Prayer: Thank you God for favor in creating us with everything we need and placing us in an assembly of like-minded sisters. Keep us in love to nurture, encourage, and uplift. Amen.

THE ARMOR OF GOD
Tania Ambroise

Ephesians 6:11-18

Focal verse: *"And take the helmet of salvation, and the sword of the Spirit, which is the word of God."*

~Ephesians 6:17 (KJV)

I love this particular scripture for a few reasons. For one, it was introduced to me by a dear friend a couple of years ago while I was going through quite a few life changes and unfortunate situations. I was dealing with a lot of stress. I felt down and out at the time and really needed someone or something to help lift my spirits. My friend opened her Bible and read Ephesians 6:11-18 to me, where Paul talks about putting on the whole armor of God to protect against evil. I was so moved by the words of this scripture that I never forgot its power even though I did not fully understand the meaning of the scripture at first. After reading the words over a few times, I was able to understand that the Lord wants His people to use His Holy Word as armor to protect against the attacks of Satan. God wants us to live a life of prayer and peace. He wants us to have strong faith and be righteous. He wants us to stand on Truth and rely on the Holy Spirit.

That day, my friend gave me her own personal Bible to keep. I have found that the more you read your Bible, the more you will understand what our God is asking of us as a people.

Prayer: Lord God, You are wise and powerful. Thank you for your Holy Word. Equip us to use Your Word as armor so that we are shielded from life's storms. Amen.

SISTER TO SISTER
Veronica L. Price

Song

Sister to sister that's how it ought to be,
God said to love you,
And for you to love me.
We are sisters in Christ and we ought to be nice.
Sister to sister that's how it ought to be.

Sister to sister that's how it ought to be.
I'll be there for you and you'll be there for me.
We are kin in God's eyes,
And you are so dear to me.
Sister to sister that's how it ought to be.

Sister to sister that's how it ought to be
I'll pray for you and you'll pray for me.
We will give each other strength,
And each other's anchor be.
Sister to sister that's how it ought to be.

Sister to sister that's how it ought to be
I'll be there for you and you'll be there for me.
Our God holds us all,
And He helps us to stand tall.
Sister to sister that's how it ought to be.

Sister to sister that's how it ought to be. (Repeat 4-5 times then end song.)

THE GRACE OF JESUS CHRIST
Martha Ramsay

1 Peter 5:5-7
Focal verse: *"God resists the proud, But gives grace to the humble."*
~1 Peter 5:5b (NKJV)

As I sit looking out of the window, my mind goes back a few years to the time when I came down with arthritis. I recall that I did not know what to do. The doctors had told me that I would never walk again. While the news was devastating, as a minister, I knew a man called Jesus who was a healer. I knew that Jesus would be there for me and not let me down. I wanted to know why this happened to me, and I turned to God for answers. I said to my God: You healed the man who sat by the pool of Bethesda for thirty years. Lord, I cried, please heal my body. I turned my plate down and began to fast and pray. I called on my Father in heaven to touch my body and deliver me from the pain. If healed, I promised God that I would preach His Word and tell the world what He had done for me. Today, I thank Jesus Christ that I can walk without the aid of a cane. What a blessing! I give God the glory.

Prayer: Lord Jesus, we know that true wisdom comes from leaning on You. Help us to trust in Your Holy Word and seek Your face. Help us to know that through You we will find Your life-giving power and miraculous healing. Amen.

LOYAL TO THE SISTERHOOD
Carolyn R. Williams

Ruth 1:16-17

Focal verse: *"I will die where you die and will be buried there. May the Lord punish me severely if I will allow anything but death to separate us!"*

~Ruth 1:17 (NLT)

The past four years have truly tested my faith. There were days when I just wanted to scream at the top of my lungs, but I remembered that God would not give me more than I could bear. As women, we have this need to take on the problems of our loved ones, which then gives us a double dose of stress. Worse, we think we are superwomen and may keep it all bottled up inside because that's how we've been raised. This is why as Christian women we must be more sensitive to the emotional needs of our sisters. We don't always know each others' stories. We don't know what each other has been going through. Sometimes we are just in pain. We feel broken, depressed, overworked, under-appreciated, unloved, rejected, and unworthy; but we continue on because that's what women do. Naomi and Ruth were two women who loved and supported each other through difficult times. Ruth had shared loneliness, anxiety and grief with Naomi, and now that the older woman was completely alone, Ruth would stand by her.

I don't know how I would have made it without the sisters in my life praying, talking and crying with me. They gave me a smile, a hug, or a call to say: "I was thinking about you", "I see your pain" and "I'm here for you". We must be willing to minister to one another and love each other as Christ loves us. As we stand side by side with our sisters in Christ, worshiping, praying, and learning about our Savior, it makes us stronger. When we pray for each other, we know that we are not alone no matter how heavy our burdens. Together we can bear each other's burdens, bringing us closer to the Lord and our sisters in Christ. We can't call ourselves The Sisterhood if we don't love each other like sisters.

Have you loved a sister today?

Prayer: Lord, when we suffer it's easy to doubt Your love, but we thank You for the loyal sisters that You have sent into our lives to remind us how much we need You and each other. Amen.

IN HIM SHALL I LIVE

"For in him we live and move and have our being.'"

~Acts 17:28 (NIV)

HONORING WOMEN
Angelique Wharton

Statement of Occasion

We gather today because of God's love, mercy and grace. As Brooklyn Community Church, we are honored that you have joined us in our Annual Women's Day celebration.

Every day God grants us serenity and wisdom to accept His guidance, and calls us to be faithful Christian women. With serenity, wisdom and faith come an unbreakable bond—The Sisterhood, which we will dedicate today.

Today, we gather not only to recognize but also to honor outstanding women for their contributions to their home, church, and communities. It is our hope that as we honor these women, we encourage others to dedicate themselves to serve God, give back to their communities, and exemplify their beliefs in Christ as they travel on this spiritual journey, called Life.

TEACH ME HOW TO PRAY

E. Frances Reid

Matthew 6:9-13

Focal verse: *"This, then, is how you should pray."*

~Matthew 6:9 (NIV)

In August, 2012, I was admitted with excruciating pain caused by diverticulitis (intestinal disease) and gallstones to a New York hospital. I was bedridden and on morphine for three days. On the fourth day, I was slowly awakened by the morning light and thanked God for life. The curtain that separated me from the next bed, was always drawn to the foot of my bed and I was unable to see my roommate. A female family member would visit this patient and continuously cry; for the doctors gave the family no hope. The patient was terminal. Only sobbing was audible.

Several days later, as I was eating my dinner, the Holy Spirit whispered to me, "Go pray for that woman". I said, "No". I had heard that those people were atheists, and they do not believe in God. But the voice was persistent. I said, "I am afraid of rejection." The Holy Spirit said, "Don't be afraid, I AM with you." I walked over to the woman's bed and said to her daughter, "May I share a moment of prayer with you for your mother?" To my surprise, she said: "Yes, but I don't know how to pray. We are Christians, but we were persecuted for praying in Russia. I never learned how to pray." I replied, "I will teach you as I was taught."

Prayer is a simple conversation between you and God. Matthew 6:9-13 reads: "Our Father, who art in Heaven, Hallowed will be thy name, Thy kingdom come, Thy will be done on earth as it is in heaven. Give us this day, our daily bread, and forgive us our trespasses as we forgive those who trespass against us. And lead us not into temptation but deliver us from all evil. For thine is the kingdom, the power and the glory forever." Amen.

Prayer: Dear Heavenly Father, thank you for teaching us to be obedient to Your voice and providing the model on how to pray. Please allow this message to be a blessing to all. Amen.

GOD, OUR STRENGTH, OUR REDEEMER
Lois Staton-Godwin

Psalm 27:14 and Psalm 46:1

Focal Verse: *"God is our refuge and strength, a very present help in trouble."*

~Psalm 46:1 (KJV)

I cried out: "No, no, no! This can't be. There must be a mistake." My oncologist paused and gently touched my arm. He gave me a glance of understanding, and then continued explaining the surgical procedure that I would have to undergo and the subsequent recuperation period that would take 3 to 4 months. As my doctor spoke to me that day, I barely heard him. My thoughts were overloaded with confusion and disbelief. After all just a few weeks prior, I had gone to the doctor for an ailment that was totally unrelated to the doctor's present diagnostic report.

I first thought about how difficult it would be for me to manage life undergoing treatment for cancer.

I am raising my 10-year old grandson. I am enrolled in a computer job training program where one is only allowed 3 days absence or is automatically dismissed. What about my job? I am a part-time manager at an upscale neighborhood restaurant. Without the extra income, financial difficulties and stress are inevitable. Yet, the surgery was imminent.

After returning home that day, I knew that it was time to pray. Alone, and in the confines of my apartment, I surrendered my all to the Master.

Prayer: Gracious Father God, with thanks, honor and praise, I am in Your presence recognizing You as my pillar of strength and courage. Through it all, my faith will remain strong in You, and I will wait on You for I know You do not fail. Amen.

NO DOUBT

"Blessed is she who believed, for there will be a fulfillment of those things which were told her from the Lord."

~Luke 1:45 (NKJV)

DISOBEDIENCE SEPARATES US FROM GOD

L. Priscilla Hall

1 Samuel 15:22

Focal Verse: *". . . Behold, to obey is better than sacrifice. . . ."*
~1 Samuel 15:22 (KJV)

My reflections spring from 1 Samuel 15:22, which reads: "But Samuel replied, What is more pleasing to the Lord: your burnt offerings and sacrifice or your obedience to His voice? Listen! Obedience is better than sacrifice and submission is better than offering the fat of rams."

I have a problem with obedience and submission. Even when I was a child I really did not like anybody telling me what to do. To avoid being told what to do, I learned what my parents expected of me and did it before they could tell me just so that I did not have to hear it. Everyone thought I was obedient, when in fact I was just arrogant. I had a strong will masked by a facade of humility and meekness. I had and still have no need for confrontation. I listen to you and then proceed to do exactly what I want.

But failure to obey God's word, leaning on your own understanding, can get you into a world of trouble. All of my errors and major mistakes came from disobeying God. I could have avoided a lot of heartache and pain, trauma and disorder if I had just listened. The arrogance of placing my puny will against His omnipotence, pitting my finite knowledge against His infinite wisdom and omniscience, now makes me shudder and I can only thank God for his mercy. He spared me and gave me another chance to trust and obey—another chance to say, Lord, have thine own way.

Obedience is better than sacrifice, but I want to go a step further and suggest that failure to obey not only results in horrible regrets but prevents the receipt of blessings. By failing to obey, we miss gifts from God. Disobedience is sin and sin separates you from God, putting you in the wrong place and wrong frame of mind. But when we obey God, things just fall into place. And there is peace.

Prayer: Father God, we are grateful for Your love. Increase our faith, decrease our fears, heal our bodies and save our souls. Help us obey Your word. Let our eyes see the blessings You have for us. Amen.

GOD BLESS OUR CHILDREN

Kareema Johnson

1 Samuel 2:1-10

Focal Verse: *"My heart rejoices in the Lord."*

~1 Samuel 2:1 (NIV)

This passage in the Bible really resonates with me. With all that Hannah went through she still found every reason to praise God. Despite the difficulty she had being able to bear a child and the fact that she was quite old when she finally did, Hannah found strength in the Lord. In 1 Samuel 2:1-10, Hannah has been given a child and joyously she begins her prayer: "My heart rejoices in the Lord." As a single mother, I relate to Hannah. Parenting is a fulfilling, yet challenging responsibility.

I have experienced both the joys and tribulations of raising my son into adulthood. My son and I haven't been seeing eye-to-eye for quite some time now. Lately, he has stopped caring about bettering himself. He also has been very disrespectful to me, and I have had to make decisions that have left me heartbroken—like putting him out of my house. I felt it was time for him to learn that the world is not as easy as he thought it would be.

When my son left, I turned to God because I needed Him to protect my son and give me peace. As my son ventured out into the world, I learned that prayer and trust in God would carry me through difficult times. I find comfort in knowing that God keeps a hedge of protection around my son. I also kept in mind that our children ultimately belong to God, and they are on loan to us. I know that if I keep praying, God will keep delivering—and He has. My son has returned home after learning some of life's harsh lessons. While things still are not perfect, I am keeping my son in my prayers and being proactive as well. I will continue to trust in the Lord for He has never failed me.

Prayer: Dear God, thank you for blessing us with children. When our children fall short of our expectations, strengthen us and heal our hearts. We rejoice in Your goodness and mercy.

WITH PURPOSE, CONTINUE WITH GOD
D. Pulane Lucas

Acts 11:19 and Acts 11:22-24

Focal Verse: *"When he came and had seen the grace of God, he was glad, and encouraged them all that with purpose of heart they should continue with the Lord."*

~Acts 11:23 (NKJV)

One morning, a dear friend shared with me that she was losing her faith in God. She could not understand why God allowed her to be born into a life filled with so much drama, trauma, pain and suffering. Sexually abused as a child and raped as a teen, she later contracted HIV from her late husband. Yet, it was not her recent cancer diagnosis that caused her to question her faith in God; it was the racism and discrimination that she experienced while receiving radiation and chemotherapy in a facility that served a predominantly Hispanic population. Vulnerable, weak and alone, she struggled to disentangle the source of the discriminatory behavior: Was it her dark brown complexion, race, socioeconomic status, or HIV status? As she walked home alone from the treatment facility, she reflected on the conditions of her life—asking: "Why God?" With each step, her thoughts seemed to assault her faith.

In Acts 11, Jewish Christians are being persecuted for spreading the Gospel. Persecution is a sustained act to exterminate or subjugate because of race, beliefs, or religion. Ultimately, persecutors want their victims to abandon their purpose in life. In this chapter, the aim is to no longer preach about Jesus or do God's will. The aim: kill someone's faith. What is seeking to kill your faith today? What is persecuting you? The source of our persecution might not be human. It could be illness, racism, loneliness, or something else.

In Acts 11:23, Barnabas says that with purpose of heart Jewish Christians should continue with the Lord. Purpose of the heart is being clear about and committed to one thing. In this verse, that means remaining with the Lord no matter what. We, too, must have resolve about our commitment to God and remain with Him in spite of attacks and persecution. With purpose, we must hold fast to our faith in God.

Prayer: Heavenly Father, give us the resolve to continue with You no matter our circumstances. Help us to be intentional about serving you Lord. Amen.

GOD'S LOVE IS UNFAILING

" . . . I trust in God's unfailing love for ever and ever. I will praise you forever for what you have done. . ."

~Psalm 52:8 (NIV)

THAT ALL MAY BE ONE
Belinda Williams

TRIBUTE

➢ To God, Jehovah and Emmanuel… the beginning and the end. We honor you Lord for the gift of life, the trials and tribulations and the challenges of the world to learn life's lessons, but we are still standing strong.

Sisterhood Standing as One

➢ We love you Dear Lord for our maternal guardians who worked on their knees, hands, and with their minds in various fields, and occupations. Our mothers, grandmothers, Big Mamas, nanas, Gma, GG, aunts, TiTis, and guardians who made sure we had an education, clothing, food and shelter to become the confident women of today and tomorrow.

Sisterhood Standing as One

➢ We are excited and praise you God for the unseen doors that have been opened for us, on today as well as yester-year. We adore you Lord and magnify your name. We are grateful for the titles and responsibilities that we have been blessed with through our careers and professions. We do not take these blessings for granted and will not fail to help others on this Christian Journey!

Sisterhood Standing as One

➢ We bless you Lord for creating our souls, bodies and minds in Your likeness. We thank you, Lord for women who work collectively to bring forth fruits that may be pleasing to Your Kingdom.

Sisterhood Standing as One

➢ We are grateful to You, Lord for our ancestors who have paved the way. We acknowledge You, Lord, for creating courageous women trail blazers who planted laid foundations so that we may all have futures overflowing with abundance.

Sisterhood Standing as One

➤ We acknowledge our present day Sheroes who God has developed, shaped and molded to lead our society and world. We thank you Lord for allowing us to witness their struggles, contributions, talents, and accomplishments. We thank and praise you God for bonds that tie us together as one. To God be the Glory!!!

Sisterhood Standing as One

EPILOGUE

"That they all may be one. . . ."
~John 17:21 (KJV)

These words were uttered by Jesus in prayer just hours before his arrest and crucifixion. Jesus' fervent petition to God was that his followers be unified in spiritual purpose, protected from the evil one and sanctified with God's truth. This compilation of reflections from The Sisterhood captures the essence of God's answer to Jesus' prayer.

Individually, the members of the Sisterhood are courageous, compassionate and caring. Transparent and true to ourselves, our reflections describe our disappointments, missed opportunities, triumphs and growing pains. Through family struggles, health challenges and spiritual awakenings, we remain steadfast in our quest to uncover the best in ourselves implanted by God before He called the light day and the darkness night. As such, we share the tenaciousness of Fannie Lou Hamer, courageousness of Harriett Tubman, fearlessness of Queen Esther, and the poise and elegance of First Lady Michele Obama.

In the poem by author Langston Hughes entitled "Mother to Son," a mother offers pertinent and truthful advice to her son. Speaking to him about the hardships of life, she says: "Well, son, I'll tell you: Life for me ain't been no crystal stair. It's had tacks in it, and splinters, and boards torn up, and places with no carpet on the floor—bare. But all the time I'se been a-climbin' on, and reachin' landin's, and turnin' corners…."

Many of us not only relate to these words but also live them. Still, despite our individual struggles and growing pains, God is equipping us for the battles of life. Through His spirit, He orders our steps and draws us closer and closer to Jesus. We, in turn, let the enemy know that we aren't going down without a fight; and as a result, we maintain our sense of hope and our spiritual swagger. Every praise is to our God!

The Sisterhood goes beyond a shared gender; we are drawn together because of our love for God, our families and each other. Like those who have gone before us, the experiences of our lives will have ripple effects for generations to come. The ripple effects will reverberate—not so that future generations may see what we have done; but, so that they will see what God has done in us, through us and for us.

That we may be one—undivided and unbroken—for generations to come.

To God be the glory!

Rev. Pamela Stanley
Pastor for Church Administration, Brooklyn Community Church

The Writers

Tania Ambroise serves as a member of the Brooklyn Community Church Choir. She earned her high school diploma and has completed some college courses. Her life's mission is helping those in need. She plans to complete her studies and open an orphanage. Tania is a stay-at-home mom who loves raising her 4-year old son. She enjoys painting, drawing, acting and dancing. She also enjoys praising God through song, reading her Bible, and strengthening her relationship with her Lord and Savior Jesus Christ.

Leonna Brabham serves as a coordinator of the Sisterhood Book Circle at Brooklyn Community Church. She holds an associate's degree in Journalism. Her passion is writing. Leonna is the self-published author of *All I Need is a Pen*, a book of poetry. She is an administrative assistant who hopes to start her my own cleaning business. She enjoys traveling and talking and listening to people. Most of all, she adores her son.

Antonia H. Daniels serves as a member of Brooklyn Community Church Choir, Kuumba Singers, Media Ministry, Spoken Word Ministry and Law Day Committee at BCC. She has studied at Brooklyn College and holds certificates in drug treatment and maintenance. Antonia serves as a vice president of the Brooklyn Unit of Church Women United, Inc. She enjoys writing poetry, reflections and essays. She also enjoys helping people, especially young people.

Tahesha Davis is a Brooklyn Community Church Choir member and serves on the Missionary Ministry and the Music and Arts Ministry at BCC. She holds a health administration degree and is an ambulatory care assistant at Memorial Sloan Kettering Cancer Center. Tahesha enjoys singing praises unto God and spending time with her husband.

Lorraine Gamble-Lofton is a founding member of the Brooklyn Community Church and holds the positions of Deacon and official Church Photographer. She is a proud, lifelong resident of Bedford-Stuyvesant. Deacon Lorraine holds a MFA in Creative Writing from The City College of New

York. She has been employed by the NYC Department of Finance for 33 years and is a reporter for the *Communique,* CWA Local 1180's newspaper. Her pastimes are writing and photography.

L. Priscilla Hall is a founding member of Brooklyn Community Church, where she serves as Vice Chair of the Deacon Ministry, Vice President of the Sisterhood, and is a member of the BCC Choir. Deacon Priscilla is a New York State Associate Justice of the Appellate Division, Second Judicial Department.

Marilyn A. Hunte serves as the Church Clerk for the Brooklyn Community Church. She is a Deacon and a Family Ministry Leader. Deacon Marilyn also is coordinating the Youth Book Circle, a component of the Sisterhood's Mentoring Program.

Kareema Johnson serves as a coordinator of the Sisterhood Book Circle at Brooklyn Community Church. She sings in the BCC Choir and loves to write and share her poetry. Kareema loves the Lord and enjoys spending time with her children, family, and BCC family.

Jessica Leach serves as a coordinator of the Sisterhood Book Circle at Brooklyn Community Church. She holds a teaching assistant certification. Jessica is an entrepreneur and baker who recently launched a new home business called Cupcake Em Up!! She enjoys baking, writing, helping others, caring for her daughter, reading, and being a part of her BCC family.

D. Pulane Lucas is First Lady at Brooklyn Community Church. She is a founding member of BCC and President of the Sisterhood. She is an Adjunct Assistant Professor who holds masters degrees in business and theology and a PhD in Public Policy and Administration. Dr. Pulane loves spending time with her husband, Rev. Fred, and children. She enjoys serving the Lord and working with the women of BCC and her church family.

Fred Lucas is Founder and Senior Pastor of one of Brooklyn's newest and fastest-growing congregations, Brooklyn Community Church. He was born and reared in Anacostia, Southeast, Washington, DC and is a graduate of Ballou High School, Harvard University, Harvard Divinity School, and Colgate Rochester Divinity School. Preaching for 42 years, he has 67 sons and daughters in the ministry. Rev. Fred is married to D. Pulane Lucas, and he is the proud father of four children and one grandchild.

Charlene Phillips serves as Deacon and Sunday School Superintendent at Brooklyn Community Church. She received a Bachelor's Degree in Social Sciences from Long Island University. Deacon Charlene retired from the City of New York where she served as District Manager of the Bedford Stuyvesant catchments area. She enjoys reading and crafts.

Veronica L. Price serves as a minister at Brooklyn Community Church. She is President of the Family Ministry at Brooklyn Community Church, and a member of the BCC choir. She holds a Master's Degree in Nursing Administration and a Master's Degree in Business Administration. She is a Registered Nurse and currently works as a Health Care Consultant. Minister Veronica loves the Lord and is very passionate about music. She enjoys songwriting, singing and helping others.

Martha Ramsay serves on the ministerial staff of the Brooklyn Community Church. She holds a bachelor's degree in Psychology, master's degrees in Nursing and Divinity, and a Doctorate of Divinity. Rev. Ramsay is the Founder and CEO of the Brooklyn Community Chaplaincy Academy in 2006.

E. Frances Reid is a founding member of Brooklyn Community Church. She serves on the Missionary Ministry, Evangelism Ministry, and Fundraising Committee, and also teaches Sunday School. She holds a PhD from Fordham University in Educational Leadership Administration and Policy/ Christian Education and is a Fordham University International Scholar. Dr. Reid enjoys spending time with her grandson.

Hattie Smith-Harris is a member of the Brooklyn Community Church Missionary Ministry. She enjoys attending Bible Study and Sunday School. As a retiree, Hattie is spending more time with her grandchildren and fixing up her house.

Pamela Stanley serves as Pastor for Church Administration at the Brooklyn Community Church. She holds a Master of Divinity degree and will complete her Doctor of Ministry in May 2015. Rev. Pam enjoys teaching the Word of God to fellow Christians and spending time with her family.

Lois Staton-Godwin serves as a Deacon at Brooklyn Community Church. She is a Family Ministry Group Leader and a member of the Missionary Ministry and the Helping Hands Ministry. She regularly attends Sunday School. Deacon Lois has been blessed with the responsibility of raising her grandson. She enjoys plays and the theater.

Bernadine Thomas-Williams is a minister at Brooklyn Community Church. She teaches the New Members' Class and serves as the Coordinator of the Counseling Ministry. Minister Bernadine is a graduate of North Carolina Central University, holds a master's degree in Social Work from The University of Connecticut, and holds a master's degree of Professional Studies in Theology from New York Theological Seminary. Minister Bernadine loves the Lord and enjoys helping others and spending time with her family.

Vonceil Turner is a founding member of Brooklyn Community Church. She serves as a Deacon, Church Treasurer and coordinator of the Hospitality Ministry. She was employed by the NYC Human Resources Administration for 21 years. She retired in 2001 as a Medicaid Trainer. Deacon Vonceil enjoys watching all sporting events, especially football.

Angelique Wharton is a member of Brooklyn Community Church. She is currently on maternity leave from the City of New York where she serves as a school safety agent. Angelique enjoys baking, writing, bowling, helping others, caring for her children, and serving the Lord.

Belinda Williams serves as a member of the Brooklyn Community Church Praise Team, Kuumba Singers, BCC Choir, Hospitality Ministry and the Missionary Ministry. She is a graduate of City College University and Adelphi University. Belinda is presently an assistant principal and a Bank Street Principals College Masters Fellowship recipient. She loves helping people who are experiencing challenges.

Carolyn R. Williams is a Deacon and Missionary President at Brooklyn Community Church. She serves as coordinator of the Benevolence Funds and member of the BCC Choir, Praise Team and Kuumba Singers. Deacon Carolyn is also a Sunday school teacher, Auburn Shelter liaison, and BCC Emergency Response Team member. She finds joy working with the youth ministry and volunteering at PS 067. She enjoys reading, gardening, sewing and spending time with her family. Deacon Carolyn is a retired Registered Nurse, who now is happily working in God's vineyard.

Bible Translations and Abbreviations

New International Version (NIV)
King James Version (KJV)
New King James Version (NKJV)
New Living Translation (NLT)
New Revised Standard Version (NRSV)

For more information about Voices From The Sisterhood inspirational books, cards and other products, please contact us at:

Brooklyn Community Church
The Sisterhood
P.O. Box 170423
Brooklyn, NY 11217
Phone: 718-622-4500

Email: bccsisterhood@bccpraise.org
Like us on Facebook at: https://www.facebook.com/VoicesFromTheSisterhood
Facebook.com/BrooklynCommunityChurch

Printed in the United States
By Bookmasters